SHORT CIRCULAR WALKS AROUND CHESTERFIELD

by

JOHN N. MERRILL

Maps and photographs by John N. Merrill

TRAIL CREST PUBLICATIONS Ltd.,
- "from footprint to finished book."

1993

Sandia Mountains
New Mexico. USA

TRAIL CREST
PUBLICATIONS
Ltd.,
WINSTER,
MATLOCK,
DERBYSHIRE.
DE4 2DQ

 (0629) 826354
(0629) 826354

Edited, typeset, designed, paged, printed, marketed and distributed by John N. Merrill.

© Text & walks - John N. Merrill 1993
© Maps-John N. Merrill/Suncrest
Ventures Ltd., 1993.
© Photographs - John N. Merrill 1993.

First Published - November 1992.
Reprinted - September 1993

ISBN 1 874754 04 7

U.S.A.
office -
P.O.Box 124.
Santa Rosa,
New Mexico.
88435
U.S.A.

Please note - The maps in this guide are purely illustrative. You are encouraged to use the appropriate 1:25,000 O.S. map.
Meticulous research has been undertaken to ensure that this publication is highly accurate at the time of going to press. The publishers, however, cannot be held responsible for alterations, errors or omissions, but they would welcome notification of such for future editions.

Typeset in - Bookman - bold, italic and plain 9pt and 18pt.

Printed by - John N. Merrill at Milne House, Speedwell
Mill, Miller's Green, Wirksworth, Derbyshire. DE4 4BL
Cover sketch - "Linacre Reservoir" by John Creber.
© Suncrest Ventures Ltd.1993.

An all British
product.

ABOUT JOHN N. MERRILL

Born in the flatlands of Bedfordshire he soon moved to Sheffield and discovered the joy of the countryside in the Peak District, where he lives. A keen walker who travels the world exploring mountains and trails. Over the last twenty years he has walked more than 150,000 miles and worn out over sixty pairs of boots. He has written more than 120 walk guides to areas in Britain and abroad, and created numerous challenge walks which have been used to raise more than £500,000 for charity. New Mexico, USA is his second home.

CONTENTS

Page No.

INTRODUCTION

Within a ten mile radius of Chesterfield is some extremely fine walking country, rich in history, folklore with an abundance of superlative buildings. The west side, bordering the Peak District National Park, is wooded and rugged, with the Cordwell Valley, Linacre Reservoirs, Stone edge and Ashover and Cocking Tor. The eastern side is flatter where industry and mining were once prolithic. Today the ground is returned to its natural state and trails link historical sites together. In the north is Ford and the Moss Valley. Closeby is the incomparable Creswell Crags and in the south is Bolsover and its impressive castle and Hardwick Hall the masterpiece of the Elizabethan era. Close to the town is the Chesterfield Canal and a walk explores the terminus area of it, while the most southern walk explores the remains of the Pinxton arm of the Cromford Canal. The longest walk is the newly opened Archaeological Way, and like many of the walks in this guide, will come as a delightful surprise.

I lived in Dronfield for many years and had long wanted to return and walk and write about the hiking in this area. For me it has enabled me to explore again some of my favourite haunts and take different paths to them. Here then is a collection of walks rich in variety, which I hope encourages you to hike in this area of Derbyshire - you will be surprised how attractive and interesting it is.....and you will meet few people!

Happy walking!
John N. Merrill

Walkers on the Archaeological Trail on the official opening on November 1st. 1992.

The Five Pits Trail.

ABOUT THE WALKS

Whilst every care is taken detailing and describing the walk in this book, it should be borne in mind that the countryside changes by the seasons and the work of man. I have described the walk to the best of my ability, detailing what I have found on the walk in the way of stiles and signs. Obviously with the passage of time stiles become broken or replaced by a ladder stile or even a small gate. Signs too have a habit of being broken or pushed over. All the route follow rights of way and only on rare occasions will you have to overcome obstacles in its path, such as a barbed wire fence or electric fence. On rare occasions rights of way are rerouted and these ammendments are included in the next edition.

The seasons bring occasional problems whilst out walking which should also be borne in mind. In the height of summer paths become overgrown and you will have to fight your way through in a few places. In low lying areas the fields are often full of crops, and although the pathline goes straight across it may be more practical to walk round the field edge to get to the next stile or gate. In summer the ground is generally dry but in autumn and winter, especially because of our climate, the surface can be decidedly wet and slippery; sometimes even gluttonous mud!

These comments are part of countryside walking which help to make your walk more interesting or briefly frustrating. Standing in a farmyard up to your ankles in mud might not be funny at the time but upon reflection was one of the highlights of the walk!

The mileage for each walk is based on three calculations -

1. pedometer reading.
2. the route map measured on the map.
3. the time I took for the walk.

I believe the figure stated for each walk to be very accurate but we all walk differently and not always in a straight line! The time allowed for each walk is on the generous side and does not include pub stops etc. The figure is based on the fact that on average a person walks 2 1/2 miles an hours but less in hilly terrain.

THE MOSS VALLEY
& ECKINGTON - 5 MILES

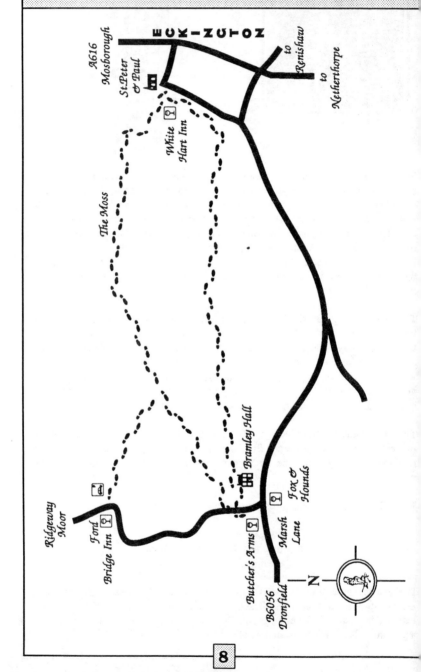

THE MOSS VALLEY & ECKINGTON
- 5 MILES

- allow 2 hours.

●● ●● ●● *Ford Car Park - Moss Valley - Bramley - Eckington -*
Moss Valley - Ford.

- 1:25,000 Pathfinder Series Sheet No. SK 48/58 Kiveton
Park and SK 47/57 - Worksop (South) & Staveley.

Start of Moss Valley at Ford - Grid Ref. 404804. Access from
near the Bridge Inn in Ford.

- Bridge Inn, Ford; just off the route at Marsh Lane is the
Butcher's Arms and the Fox & Hounds; Eckington has numerous
including The Angel, Duke of York, Prince of Wales and White
Hart.

ABOUT THE WALK - When living in Dronfield, I often walked the
Moss Valley, and has remained one of my favourite haunts of North-
East Derbyshire. It is a delightful wooded valley with remains of several
dams for here in the 18th & 19th century was a bustling scythe and
sickle industry. Eckington is well worth exploring to see many attractive buildings and the church dedicated to St.Peter and St. Paul, has
origins dating back to 1,100 A.D. Most of the walk is on well defined
footpaths and tracks with a little road walking in Eckington.

WALKING INSTRUCTIONS - From the car park at Ford, follow the
path past the dam and into the valley and in 1/4 mile cross a
footbridge. At the next footbridge, almost 1/4 mile later, at the start of
the woodland, cross it and turn right on the path that ascends. First
through woodland then along the edge of a field with the hedge on your
left, to a stile. Continue gently ascending with Bramleyhill Farm on
your right. In the top lefthand corner of the field, beside woodland, gain
a track and follow this beside the wood on your left. Soon it turns left
then sharp right and brings you to minor road from Ridgeway with

Habberjam Farm on your right. Turn left and in a few yards left again along the farm drive to the Hall; footpath signed. If you continued along the road for a few more yards you reach Marsh Lane and the Butcher's Arms and Fox & Hounds Inn.

Walk past the hall to a gate and leave the track and follow a distinct path to another gate. Basically you keep straight ahead all the time - walking due east towards Eckington - and the path becomes a magnificent hedged path with a rugby field on your right. Little over 1/2 mile from the farm you emerge onto a track with houses on your right. Keep ahead on the track and in 1/4 mile pass a school on your right. Just afterwards walk along Stead Street, then Pinfold Street to the main road in Eckington. Continue ahead passing The Angel Inn and Duke of York Inn to your right, then the Prince of Wales Inn - very patriotic here! - and onto the White Hart Inn. Here leave the road to walk along Mill Road on the right of the White Hart Inn and parish church on your right. Follow the narrow road past Church Farm and down to The Moss brook and weir. Just afterwards turn left onto a track and begin walking up the Moss Valley. For the first 1/2 mile keep straight ahead on the track, away from the brook and with Ladybank Wood on your right. After 1/2 mile as you approach woodland - Cadman Wood - turn left on a footpath to a footbridge. Cross The Moss and turn right and now walk along the lefthand side of the valley with the remains of the dams on your right. Where the track/path divides keep right and continue in the valley and in 1/4 mile reach the footbridge you crossed earlier. Cross it again and retrace your steps for the final 1/2 mile back to the car park at Ford.

Pinxton Wharf and canal - see Pinxton walk.

REMEMBER AND OBSERVE THE COUNTRY CODE

Enjoy the countryside and respect its life and work.

Guard against all risk of fire.

Fasten all gates.

Keep your dogs under close control.

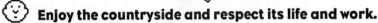 **Keep to public paths across farmland.**

Use gates and stiles to cross fences, hedges and walls.

Leave livestock, crops and machinery alone.

Take your litter home - pack it in; pack it out.

Help to keep all water clean.

Protect wildlife, plants and trees.

Take special care on country roads

Make no unnecessary noise.

HOLMESFIELD
& CORDWELL - 6 MILES

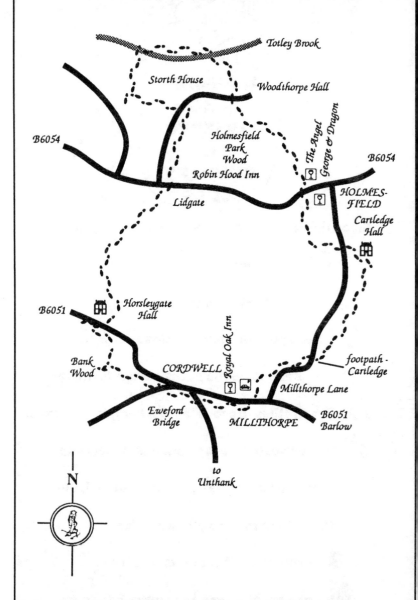

MILLTHORPE LANE - is said to be haunted by a ghost who sits astride a white horse at midnight!

HOLMESFIELD
& CORDWELL
- 6 MILES
- allow 2 to 2 1/2 hours.

- Cordwell - Cartledge - Holmesfield - Holmesfield Park Wood - Woodthorpe Hall - Totley Brook - Storth House - Lidgate - Horsleygate Hall - Bank Wood - Eweford Bridge - Cordwell.

- 1:25,000 Pathfinder Series Sheet No. 761 (SK 36/37) - Chesterfield.

- Millthorpe Lane, Cordwell. Grid Ref. SK318764. Close to the junction with the B6051 road near the Royal Oak Inn in Cordwell.

- Royal Oak Inn, Cordwell; George & Dragon, The Angel, Holmesfield; Robin Hood Inn, Lidgate.

ABOUT THE WALK - An outstanding walking area just outside the Peak District National park and Sheffield city boundary. In June the western end of the Cordwell Valley is a riot of colour with the rhoderdendrons out in full bloom. The walk can be extended to fully appreciate this array. The circuit takes you through woodland and past historic halls and rolling countryside, with two ascents and descents.

WALKING INSTRUCTIONS - From the car park walk up Millthorpe Lane following the road round to your right and where it turns left, leave it on your right, as footpath signed - "Cartledge". Keep to the lefthand drive and walk past a house to a stile on the edge of the garden. The path is now defined and keeps beside the wall on your right to a walled track. Follow this past Cartledge Hall Farm into Cartledge Lane and follow it round to your left, with the two Cartledge Hall's on your right. Gaining the lane - Millthorpe Lane - turn left then right, as footpath signed - "Unthank 1 1/4 miles." At first it is a track and descend to a stile and continue descending to a footbridge. Turn right after crossing it to a stile and ascend the field with the hedge on your left to Holmesfield, gaining the main road via the George & Dragon Inn, opposite St. Swithin's church.

13

Turn left then right along Park Avenue; footpath signed - "Woodthorpe Hall & Totley" - on the immediate lefthand side of The Angel Inn. Walk along the lane passing Hall Farm on your left and where the drive enters a private house, use the stile on the right and follow the path along the edge of a field into Holmesfield Park Wood. Basically keep straight ahead through the wood, following a path at first then a track and in 1/2 mile reach the road, just south of Woodthorpe Hall. Follow the road for a few yards to a footpath sign and kissing gate on your left. Turn left and keep the hedge on your right as you descend to a stile. Continue to two more before descending a field to the edge of woodland surrounding Totley Brook - the boundary of Derbyshire & South Yorkshire. Ignore the stile on your left and bear right along the path to a footbridge over the brook. Cross this and soon gain a wide path; turn left along this, through the woodland and brook on your left. Keep on this for a 1/3 mile - about 8 minutes walking - until you reach a path on your left. Turn left along this to a footbridge and cross the brook. Gaining a field aim for the lefthand corner - the path is little used - Here bear left then right following a track, which you soon leave as you ascend towards the righthand side of Storth House. Using the stile gain the farm drive and turn right then left along a track. Immediately past the building turn left at a stile and walk past them and down to a small pond on your right. Cross a stile and ascend the slope to minor road near Fanshaw Gate. Turn right along the narrow road to the B6054 road at Lidgate. To your left is the Robin Hood Inn.

Go straight across to a stile and footpath sign - "Horsleygate Hall " - in memory of Victor Reed. The path is well stiled and visible as you cross the fields and descend towards the lefthand side of the hall. In the last field keep to your lefthandside as signed to reach a stile in the bottom before the road. Turn right along the road past the Hall to the B6051 road. Turn right along it for 1/4 mile to a gate and footpath sign on your left. You are now well into the Cordwell Valley and if you continue a little further you will see the array of rhoderdendrons. Turn left through the gate and into woodland. Follow the wide path round to your left and at the first fork keep left and continue through the wood - Bank Wood - into a field and cross a footbridge before gaining the B6051 road, via a stile beside a path sign - "Fox Lane Top". Turn right and follow the B6051 road to Eweford Bridge and onto Cordwell village and the Royal Oak Inn, near to where you began.

CARTLEDGE HALL - dates from the 17th century. It is unusual to see two impressive halls side by side. According to a legend two brothers lived in the earlier hall but constantly argued with the younger brother bearing the brunt of the argument. One day, during an argument the younger brother heard music in another room and left to investigate. He found nothing but a voice told him - *"thy duty is to leave this place and build a house elsewhere."* He did, building one opposite blocking his brother's view!

The two Cartledge Hall's.

OLD WHITTINGTON
& UNSTONE - 6 MILES

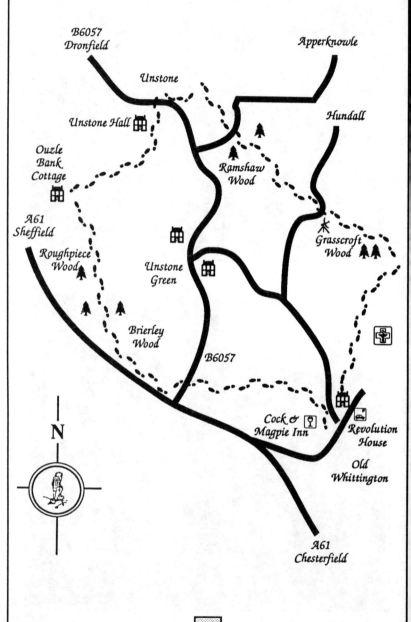

B6057
Dronfield

Apperknowle

Unstone

Unstone Hall

Hundall

Ouzle
Bank
Cottage

Ramshaw
Wood

A61
Sheffield

Roughpiece
Wood

Grasscroft
Wood

Unstone
Green

Brierley
Wood

B6057

Cock &
Magpie Inn

Revolution
House

Old
Whittington

N

A61
Chesterfield

OLD WHITTINGTON
& UNSTONE
- 6 MILES

- allow 2 to 2 1/2 hours.

 *- Revolution House, Old Whittington - Brierley Wood - Ouzle Bank Cottage - Unstone Hall - B6057 - Ramshaw Wood - Mast - Grasscroft Wood - Revolution House, Old Whittington.*

 1:25,000 Pathfinder Series Sheet No. 761 (SK 36/37) - Chesterfield.

- Roadside parking near Revolution House, Old Whittington.

- Cock & Magpie Inn, Old Whittington.

ABOUT THE WALK - Revolution House is well worth visiting - open from Easter to October - to see where history was made, leading to the Glorious Revolution of 1688. The walk itself passes through surprisingly attractive countryside on the northern side of Chesterfield. Taking you through woodland to an impressive hall before ascending over fields and beside woodland to regain Old Whittington.

WALKING INSTRUCTIONS - Walk up the road - leading to Unstone Green - on the left of Revolution House, passing the Cock & Magpie Inn. After a few yards with a school on your right turn left along a footpath on the right of the house - West Garth. The path leads to a stile and open fields. Continue ahead into a large field and in a few yards the path turns left then right and descends to a stile in the hedge. In the next field keep the hedge on your right before crossing the open field to a stile above the railway line. Over this turn left and descend to a footbridge over the line. Just afterwards bear left along the path passing a factory and emerging onto the B6057 road opposite a former chapel. Turn right then left along the road to the Dronfield by pass. After a few yards turn right onto a tarmaced track leading to Brierley Wood. Go through a gate at the top and a few yards later bear right and ascend through a former quarry area onto a defined track in the wood. In 1/4 mile it divides; keep to the righthand one with a fence on your right. About a 1/3 mile later keep to the righthand path along the perimeter of the wood. Ahead you can see your destination - **Ouzle Bank Cottage.**

Just before the cottage - Ouzle Bank Farm 1915 - turn right at the stile. Walk past the farm on your left to another stile and continue with the field boundary right to a stile. Here bear left for a few yards then right descending the field with the hedge on your left. Follow the hedge round to your left and reach Unstone Hall. Walk down the farm drive to the B6057 road with the railway bridge on your right. Turn right and walk under the bridge and turn left, as footpath signed, passing the former Old Horse & Jockey. To your right is a car complex. Walk along the path and cross the River Drone and ascend steps. At the top turn right along the line of a former railway line in woodland. Follow the distinct path passing a playing field on your right, as it curves to your left to minor Unstone/Apperknowle road. Turn right and in a few yards, immediately after crossing the railway line, turn left, as footpath signed, and descend to a track junction beside the house "Siscar." Turn left along the track towards Ramshaw Lodge. Approaching the Ramshaw Wood, leave the track on your left to a footbridge and cross the former railway line, again. Continue up the field to a kissing gate, with Woodsmithies Farm to your left.

Turn right on the hedged path and where it divides bear left and ascend round to your left and follow the defined path keeping close to the field edge on your left to a lane and prominent mast, 1/4 mile away. Turn right then left, as footpath signed and continue with the field boundary on your left to a stile. Walk through a few yards of Grasscroft Wood to another stile and for the next three fields keep the wood's perimeter on your right. In the third field the wood juts out and here turn right onto a track and walk through the wood to open fields - views to Old Whittington & Chesterfield. On your right is a pond. Bear half left across the field, aiming for its middle to find a stile. Continue to another, fringed by woodland on your left, around a hospital. Keep the field boundary on your immediate left and after two fields gain a footbridge. Cross it and follow the path round to your left to a cemetery on your right. Here turn right on the path beside it, following the well defined path back to Cock & Magpie Inn and Revolution House.

REVOLUTION HOUSE - formerly the Cock and Pynot Inn - pynot being the local name for magpie. Here in June 1688, the 4th Earl of Devonshire, The Earl of Danby and John D'Arcy, hatched a plan that culminated in the Glorious Revolution in November 1688, William of Orange became the King of England. In May 1694 the Earl of Devonshire was made a Duke for his participation in the event.

Revolution House.

Unstone Hall.

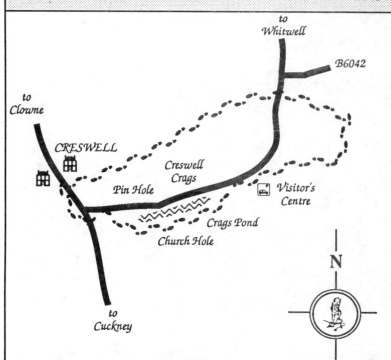

Creswell Crags.

CRESWELL CRAGS
- 3 MILES
- allow 1 1/4 hours

Location - *Just east of the village of Creswell on the B6042 road, on the Derbyshire/Nottinghamshire boundary in The Dukeries.*

1:25,000 Pathfinder - Sheet No SK47/57 - Worksop (South) & Staveley

and start -   Grid Reference SK539744. Parking at Creswell Crags Visitor's Centre, just off the B6042 road. Note - the car park closes at 5 p.m. daily.

Character - *well defined level tracks and paths throughout. Good shoes advised; can be wet in winter.*

toilets, refreshments and visitor's information at the car park. Further facilities of shops , restaurants and inns in Creswell nearby.

ABOUT THE WALK - Creswell Crags is an impressive limestone gorge with numerous caves where remains of man and animals dating back to the ice-age have been found. The visitors centre has an exhibition on the discovery and history of early that once occupied the site. The Derbyshire/Nottinghamshire boundary runs through the middle of the gorge, which has a road, stream and large pond. The walk is on well defined paths - half in woodland and half beside fields. There is only a few feet of ascent and is certainly a family walk with plenty of interest and exploration, including wild flowers and bird life, in the woods and lake area. There is no pub on the walk but refreshments can be had at the visitor's centre. The walk should take 1 to 1 1/2 hours to complete.

WALKING INSTRUCTIONS - The walk begins at the Creswell Crags Visitor's Centre car park and is walked in an anti-clockwise direction. Walk along the track away from the Centre and road to a bar gate in approximately 100 yards. Turn left, as bridlepath signed, and follow a well defined farm track (to Hennymoor Farm). Just before the first field boundary (hedge) on your left, turn left and follow the grass track keeping the hedge on your right to a small gate and bridlepath sign at the minor road. Turn left and in 10 yards turn right onto another bridlepath with a metal bar gate. Keep on this well defined track for little over 1/2 miles (0.6 km). Turn left beside the A616 road on the outskirts of Creswell village. Turn left along Crags Road (B6042). At the traffic lights turn right onto the path around Crags Pond. Walk clockwise around the pond, duplicating the lefthand side path at the end to reach the opposite of the pond. Follow path down the steps with the stream on your right to the Visitor's Centre and car park.

CRESWELL CRAGS - The limestone crags that lie either side of the narrow gorge, which also acts of the boundary of Derbyshire and Nottinghamshire, is one the main places in Britain to study paleontology - the study of fossils. The caves in the limestone cliffs, of which there are five major ones, have been home to early man since about 43,000 B.C. The walk takes you through very pleasant woodland before curving round to enter the gorge and see the caves and pond. As the caves lie on either side of the pond you walk around the lake to see them at close hand. The Visitor's Centre has a display about the gorge and the finds it has revealed. The public are not allowed to explore the caves and metal grids across their openings prevent access. The gorge is a Site of Special Scientific Interest (SSSI) for its geology and natural history. A variety of wild flowers and birds will be seen on the walk and the caves are home to bats.

WELBECK ABBEY - The crags and pond were once part of the Welbeck Estate, whose origins date back several hundred years. In 1538 Welbeck Abbey was the seat of the White Canons of the Premonstratensian Order. Later the land came into the Shrewsbury and Cavendish family who owned the nearby Bolsover Castle and Hardwick Hall. The Abbey is now Welbeck College and the impressive house and estate is mostly the work of the Dukes of Portland. The riding school, as with the whole building, is on a grand scale measuring 385 feet long by 112 feet wide.

CRAGS POND - Just up the road you passed Crags Cottage which was once the old Star Inn and the last building of a small settlement by a watermill here at the southern end of the pond. In the 1700's the Duke of Portland engaged the painter George Stubbs to paint views of the Welbeck Estate. One known as, "Two Gentlemen Going Shooting" shows the mill and crags. The mill and thatched buildings were demolished in the 1860's as part of an extensive landscaping programme of the estate. The mill pond was drained and the present lake was made by damming the stream, to create a duck shooting lake for the Duke's enjoyment.

PIN HOLE CAVE - named after a 19th century custom of each visitor placing a pin in the rock pool near the entrance. Excavations earlier this century have uncovered more than 15,000 pieces of bone. Evidence confirms that man has occupied the cave intermittently over the last 45,000 years, and hyenas used it as a den.

ROBIN HOOD'S CAVE - the largest cave with four main chambers.

MOTHER GRUNDY'S PARLOUR - named after a witch who lived here last century, the cave. The cave has yielded many interesting bones and intriguing study of the life of early man.

BOAT HOUSE CAVE - so named as the boat for the lake was kept here. When the lake level was lowered in the 1930's the cave was extensively excavated but few items were uncovered, just bones of hyena, bison and horse.

CHURCH HOLE CAVE - The cave extends 170 feet into the hillside and has yielded the finest artifacts from the area. Hyena's used it as their lair and bones from bison, bear, wolf, woolly rhinoceros, horse and cave lion. The cave has been occupied by Neanderthal man with stone implements found, and pottery fragments show that it was occupied in both Roman and mediaeval times.

Hiker's on the Creswell Archaeological Trail.

THE CRESWELL ARCHAEOLOGICAL WAY - 13 MILES END TO END.

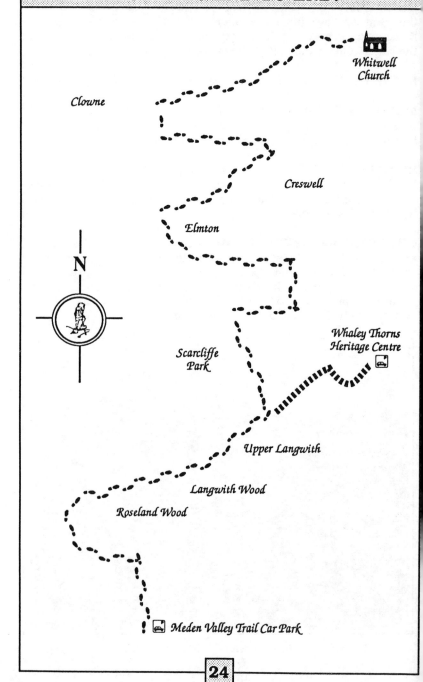

Whitwell Church

Clowne

Creswell

Elmton

N

Whaley Thorns Heritage Centre

Scarcliffe Park

Upper Langwith

Langwith Wood

Roseland Wood

Meden Valley Trail Car Park

THE CRESWELL ARCHAEOLOGICAL WAY

- 13 MILES - end to end.
- allow 5 hours or more.

- Meden Valley Trail car park near Pleasley Mill to Whitwell Church via Roseland Wood - Langwith Wood - Upper Langwith - (Whaley Thorns detour) - Whaley - Elmton - Clowne - Whitwell.

1:25,000 Pathfinder Series, Sheet Nos. SK 47/57 and SK 46/56.

- Meden Valley Trail , Grid Ref. SK510649.

Numerous along the trail; the first at Upper Langwith - the Devonshire Arms.

ABOUT THE WALK - I had the honour and pleasure to officially open this trail on November 1st 1992. Together with about 130 walkers we hiked the first six miles of the trail to Whaley Thorns Heritage Centre. The centre is well worth a visit to see the farm sections; the mining section and the archaeological section; all of which enhances your understanding and appreciation of the area and trail. The trail is well signed with a gold waymark and passes through attractive scenery - on the Derbyshire, Nottinghamshire and South Yorkshire boundaries - through woodland and fields, passing numerous places of historical and archaeological interest. You can hike the route end to end - if there is a party of you doing it you can leave one car at Whitwell for your return back to Meden Vale. Alternatively you can walk it in sections.

The inspiration for the trail and much of the work has been done by the Creswell Groundwork Trust. They have produced an informative route sheet to the way with instructions and history notes. Further information can be obtained from -

Whaley Thorns Heritage Centre, Cockshutt Lane,
Whaley Thorns, Langwith, Nottinghamshire. NG20 9HA
Tel. 0623 - 742525

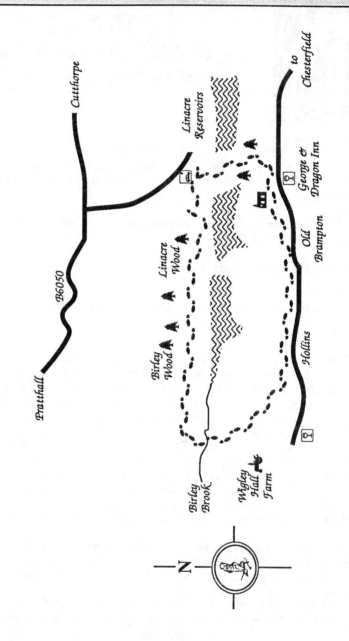

LINACRE
RESERVOIRS &
OLD BRAMPTON
- 4 MILES
- Allow 1 1/2 to 2 hours.

- Linacre Reservoir car park - Linacre Wood - Hollins - Old Brampton - Linacre Reservoir.

 - 1:25,000 Pathfinder Series Sheet No. 791 (SK36/37) - Chesterfield

 - Linacre Reservoir Grid Ref. SK335728.

- George & Dragon Inn, Old Brampton.

ABOUT THE WALK - Linacre three reservoirs are a jewel, situated four miles east of Chesterfield. First you walk beside the upper two through woodland to fields in a shallow valley. You ascend by a wooded stream and fields to the minor road at Hollins. All the time having extensive views to the reservoirs. You follow the lane into Old Brampton where there is an inn and one of the most interesting church's in Derbyshire. The final section is down the fields from the church to the dam wall of the lowest of the reservoirs before regaining the car park. The walk is delightful mixture of water, wood and views.

WALKING INSTRUCTIONS - From the car park descend the wooden steps to a track and turn right along it walking through woodland and soon gaining the righthand side of the middle reservoir. Continue on the track to the dam wall of the upper reservoir. Here bear right then left following the gravel path through Linacre Wood. Cross a wooden footbridge over a side stream and continue to the western end of the reservoir and another footbridge. Here leave the gravel track and keep straight ahead on a small path through the trees to a stile on the perimeter of the wood. Turn left keeping near the wall on your left to some stepping stones. Now in a shallow valley continue along its base with the stream to your left to a stone slab across it and a wooded hollow beyond. Ascend through the trees on the defined path to the top. Here turn left beside the wall to reach a stile. Over this keep the field boundary on your immediate left and at the end of the field gain another stile. Keep the wall on your left and look out for another stile halfway along the field. Over this keep the wall on your right to the next stile. Well to your right is Wigley. Continue to another stile on the right of a gate. Shortly afterwards is a large wooden stile and here turn left following the lefthand side of the field to another stile. Cross a small field to a stile with a house and garage on your right and gain the minor road via a stile by a footpath sign. Turn left along the road passing Hollins House almost immediately.

Continue on the road for 1/2 mile to the attractive village of Old Brampton and its church dedicate to St. Peter and St. Paul. Continue to the George & Dragon Inn and turn left through the lynch gate and walk through the churchyard to the right of the church. At the end gain a stile and keep ahead across the fields beside the lefthand boundary to more stiles. In the last field before the wood around Linacre Reservoirs, the path goes diagonally right across the field to a stile and footpath sign. Alternatively you go through the stile on your left and turn right along the defined path which curves to your right and meets the other path in 250 yards. Here turn left and descend to the dam wall of the lowest dam. Cross over and ascend the steps to the road. Turn right to the toilet block and turn left and ascend the road back to the car park.

OLD BRAMPTON CHURCH - dedicated to St. Peter and St. Paul dates back to Norman times, is well worth exploring. The south aisle walls have 13th century sculptures let into the walls. The tower supports an octagonal tower - a broach spire.

Linacre Reservoir.

Linacre Reservoir.

Old Brampton church.

CHESTERFIELD &
THE CHESTERFIELD CANAL
- 4 1/4 MILES

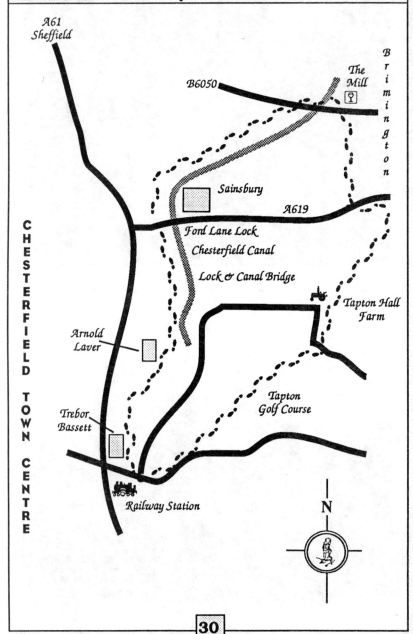

A61 Sheffield

B6050

Brimington

The Mill

Sainsbury

A619

Ford Lane Lock

Chesterfield Canal

Lock & Canal Bridge

Tapton Hall Farm

Arnold Laver

Tapton Golf Course

Trebor Bassett

Railway Station

CHESTERFIELD TOWN CENTRE

N

CHESTERFIELD &
THE CHESTERFIELD
CANAL
- 4 1/2 MILES

- allow 1 1/2 to 2 hours.

- Ford Lane Lock - Chesterfield Canal - B6050 - Brimington - A619 - Tapton Hall Farm - Tapton Golf Course - Chesterfield Railway Station - River Rother - Chesterfield Canal - Ford Lane Lock.

- 1:25,000 Pathfinder Series Sheet No. 761 (SK 36/37) - Chesterfield.
- 1:25,000 Pathfinder Series Sheet No. SK 47/57 - Worksop (South) & Staveley.

- Roadside parking on Ford Lane - Grid Ref. SK388729.

- The Mill Inn, B6050, Brimington.

ABOUT THE WALK - The Chesterfield Canal is fascinating and well worth walking in its its own right. I have detailed several walks along the canal in my Canal series - Vol. 1 - Derbyshire & Nottinghamshire. Over the last few years the Chesterfield Canal Society have "rescued" the canal from oblivion and now major strides are afoot to restore the "un-navigitable section" from Chesterfield to Worksop. This walk takes from a restored lock along the canal a short distance to the north before walking south to gain central Chesterfield and the start of the canal. You follow the canal back to Ford Lane Lock. An outstanding walk although situated in the town's environment! Like all canals the towpath provides a natural haven away from modern life.

WALKING INSTRUCTIONS - Descend to the lock and walk under the canal bridge, heading northwards - you are following a section of the Cuckoo Way - along the towpath and 45 miles to West Stockwith and the junction with the River Trent. The towpath curves to your right passing Sainsbury's on your right and 1/4 mile later the Greyhound

Stadium. 1/4 mile later reach the B6050 Brimington road, opposite The Mill Inn. Turn right up the road for a few yards to the end of a row of houses to No. 165 - Mulberry House. Here turn right along the track with a wood on your left. At the end of the wood is a stile on your left and turn left and soon gain the road Woodlands. Follow it to its junction with Landsdowne Road and turn right, following this road to the A619 - Stavely Road. Turn left and ascend it passing the cemetery on your right. Little over 1/4 mile later pass Almond Place, dated 1852, on your left. Just after turn right into Briar View and keep to the righthand track leading to a car wreckers compound - Ivy House Farm. Here is a stile and continue along the field boundary on your right to another. Here angle right and descend the field to a footbridge. Cross and ascend the otherside, on a good path to a wood where bear left to lane close to Tapton Hall Farm.

Turn right then left, as stiled, and pass the farm on your immediate right to another stile. Continue ahead to a lane where bear left along it for less than 1/4 mile, to a lefthand bend with a bridlepath sign and track on your right. Turn right along this and follow this well signed path through Tapton Golf Course, past the Club House and down the drive to road. Keep straight ahead down this curving down to your right towards Chesterfield Railway Station. Pass under the railway line and turn right over the bridge over the River Rother. Turn left keeping the river on your left and passing a row of houses on your right to the old Stavely Road. Turn left then right along Holbeck Close, with the River Rother now on your right. On your left is Trebor Bassett and in a few yards reach a Chesterfield Canal Information board. Continue now on a well defined path and in 200 yards cross a footbridge and keep the river on your left; on your right is Arnold Laver's. In 1/4 mile gain a canal bridge and lock - where the canal leaves the river. Just after you are walking with the canal on your right and the river below on your left. Pass under Tapton Tunnel 1A and regain Ford Lane Lock.

THE CHESTERFIELD CANAL - The canal - 46 miles long with 65 locks - was completed on June 4th 1777 at a cost of £152,000. The construction of the Norwood Tunnel - 2,850 yards long - was a a major undertaking and in the long term brought about the demise of the canal, as it constantly needed attention and suffered from roof collapse and subsidence. In 1848 200,000 tons was being carried by the canal but ten years later it was half this amount. The railways took the business away and in 1908 the Norwood tunnel was closed. The section from Worksop to West Stockwith and the River Trent is still in use by pleasure craft. As will be seen on this walk the canal is being restored.

Chesterfield Canal bridge and lock, near start of the canal.

Ford Lane Lock.

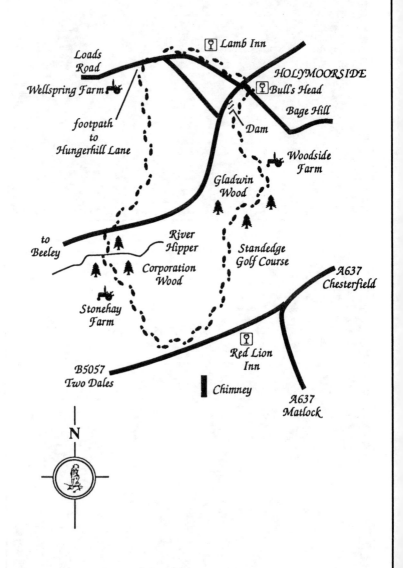

HOLYMOORSIDE
&
STANDEDGE
- 4 MILES
- allow 1 1/2 to 2 hours.

- - - *- Holymoorside - Loads Road - Nab Quarry - River Hipper - Corporation Wood - Stonehay Farm - Stone Edge - Standedge Golf Course - Gladwin Wood - Woodside Farm - Bage Hill - Holymoorside.*

- 1:25,000 Pathfinder Series Sheet No. 778 (SK26/36) - Bakewell and Matlock.

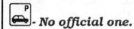

- No official one.

Bull's Head and Lamb Inn, Holymoorside. Just off the route at Stone Edge - Red Lion Inn.

ABOUT THE WALK - Holymoorside is an attractive village with many houses worth looking at. The walk takes you through rugged country-side and across the River Hipper, surprisingly attractive, full of woodland and gritstone rocks as you ascend to Stone Edge. Here you descend past Standedge Golf Course, back into woodland as you return to Holymoorside via Woodside Farm and a small dam. A very rewarding wooded walk.

WALKING INSTRUCTIONS - Starting from the road junction beside the Bull's Head in Holymoorside. Cross the road and walk up Loads Road and bear left - still on Loads Road - passing the Lamb Inn on your right. Continue on the road, ascending gently, for 1/3 mile past the houses to a footpath sign - "Hungerhill Lane" and fenced path on your left, near Wellspring Farm. Turn left along the path which soon becomes a walled track and in a 1/3 mile gain the edge of the "Hipper Valley". Follow the path to your right as it descends diagonally down the slope with views of wooded valley. At the bottom reach a minor road by a footpath sign and turn right. After a few yards turn left at the footpath sign near a gate and gain a track. Follow this down to the River Hipper and footbridge on your left. Cross over and begin ascending the other side on a distinct rocky path through woodland for 1/4 mile. After a stile join a track at Stonehay Farm and follow this gently uphill to the road - B5057 - at Stone Edge.

Turn left and after a few yards opposite the telephone kiosk turn left along the road to Standedge Golf Club. To your right is the solitary chimney of the Stone Edge lead smelting complex - the best preserved in Derbyshire. Further along the road is the Red Lion Inn. Follow the golf course road down and around to the club house 1/2 mile away. Continue past the club house and farm to a footpath sign and turn left keeping to the edge of the fairway to another sign. Here bear right and leave the golf course and descend through woodland on a good path. In 1/4 mile you walk along the perimeter of Gladwin Wood, past pine trees to a stile and track beyond. Turn right along the track to Woodside Farm and just before it bear left and follow the path along the righthand side of the field to a slab bridge. Continue on the path and where it divides keep on the lefthand one and soon pass Holymoorside Dam on your left. Just after gain a minor road inbetween two chapels, near Bage Hill. Turn left and in a few more strides you are back at the road junction beside the Bull's Head Inn in central Holymoorside.

Lamb Inn, Holymoorside.

36

Chimey and site of lead-smelting complex, Stone Edge.

Holymoorside Dam.

BOLSOVER &
SCARCLIFFE - 4 1/2 MILES

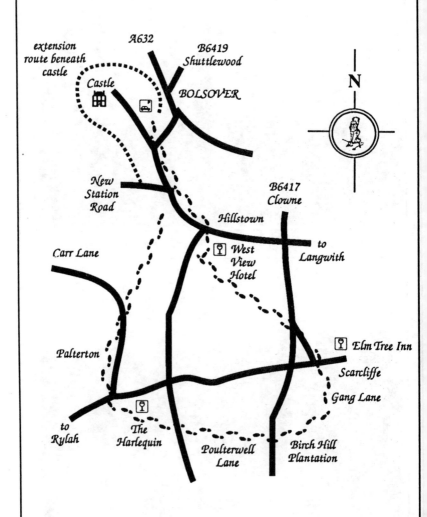

extension
route beneath
castle

A632

B6419
Shuttlewood

Castle

BOLSOVER

N

New
Station
Road

B6417
Clowne

Hillstown

Carr Lane

West
View
Hotel

to
Langwith

Palterton

Elm Tree Inn

Scarcliffe

Gang Lane

to
Rylah

The
Harlequin

Poulterwell
Lane

Birch Hill
Plantation

BOLSOVER
&
SCARCLIFFE
- 4 1/2 MILES
- allow 2 hours.

 *- Bolsover - Hillstown - Scarcliffe - Gang Lane - Birch Hill Plantation - Poulterwell Lane - Palterton - Hillstown - Bolsover.*

 1:25,000 Pathfinder Series Sheet Nos. SK 47/57 - Worksop (South) & Staveley and SK 46/56 - Mansfield (North) and part of Sherwood Forest.

- Castle Street, Bolsover.

- Blue Bell Inn, Bolsover; West View Hotel, Hillstown; Elm Tree Inn, Scarcliffe - just off the route; The Harlequin, Palterton.

ABOUT THE WALK - Bolsover is a most attractive walking area, with the impressive castle standing proud over the Vale of Scarsdale. I never tire of walking here for there is much to see and explore; the paths are defined and the views extensive. You can extend the walk to walk around the castle via Castle Lane and a footpath beneath its ramparts - adding 1/2 mile to the walk. The castle is well worth exploring; Bolsover parish church has a chapel to the Cavendish family; closeby is the towns earthwork; Scarcliffe has an interesting church with a monument to Lady Constantia and the curfew bell is still rung; and the ridge walk from Palterton has extensive views westwards to the ruins of Sutton Scarsdale Hall and southwards to the towers of Hardwick Hall.

WALKING INSTRUCTIONS - Walk up to the main road - High Street - from the car park and turn left. Pass the Blue Bell Inn on your right and the parish church on your left. At the road junction just afterwards continue ahead on Langwith Road passing the town's earthwork on your left. The road curves round to your left and on the right of the bend is the path you will be returning on from Palterton. Continue round the bend and turn right onto the Mansfield Road. In a few yards pass the West View Hotel on your left. On the right of it is the footpath sign. Leave the road here and cross the playing field with the Ace of Clubs on your left. Aim for the far righthand corner of the field. From here the path is defined as you cross the fields towards Scarcliffe. In 1/2 mile approach a flat mound and keep to the lefthand side of it and just afterwards reach a track. Turn left along it for a few yards to a stile on your right. Continue across two stiled fields to a road junction. Cross over to the minor road and follow this into Scarcliffe.

At the main road in Scarcliffe turn left then right, close to a telephone kiosk, into a lane that soon becomes a track - Gang Lane. Before turning right if you continue to your left you will reach Scarcliffe church. Follow the track for 1/4 mile until you reach the final field on your right before Birch Hill Plantation. Turn right through a stile and cross the field towards its far righthand corner, where a gap in the perimeter wall of the plantation, gives access to a footpath. Follow this round to your right to a wider path and follow this to the Mansfield Road, by a footpath sign. Cross the road and follow the track opposite - bridlepath signed - Poulterwell Lane. The track is well defined and follow it due west for over 1/2 mile to the road junction on the eastern side of Palterton. Go straight across and walk along Main Street, passing The Harlequin Inn on your right. Continue to the edge of the vale and turn right - still on Main Street. Walk past the houses on your right and the aptly named road "Pennine View". Where the road starts to descend keep straight ahead, as footpath signed, to a kissing gate. Continue across a field passing The Elms Farm on your right. Beyond reach a stile and walk along the crest of the vale on a well defined path. Walk past Valley View on your left and past the houses of Hillstown to the road you walked along earlier. Continue ahead on Langwith Road and retrace your steps back to the car park in Bolsover. If wanting to walk around the castle, turn left down Castle Lane and in 30 yards turn right and follow the footpath beneath the castle to the main road. Here turn right to regain the shopping area and car park of Bolsover.

BOLSOVER CASTLE - Origins of the castle date back to Norman times, but most of the present building dates from the 17th century. The keep, Long Gallery, and Riding Stables were built in the early 17th century by Sir William Cavendish, who became the Earl of Mansfield and the Duke of Newcastle. In 1644 the Royalists and Parliamentarians occupied the building during the Civil War. In 1755 it belonged to the Duke of Portland who stripped the roofs and took the material for use in the building of Welbeck Abbey. In 1945 the partially ruined buildings were given to the then Ministry of Works and in more recent times considerable restoration work has been carried out at this most impressive building.

THE HIKER'S CODE

✿ Hike only along marked routes - do not leave the trail.

✿ Use stiles to climb fences; close gates.

✿ Camp only in designated campsites.

✿ Carry a light-weight stove.

✿ Leave the trail cleaner than you found it.

✿ Leave flowers and plants for others to enjoy.

✿ Keep dogs on a leash.

✿ Protect and do not disturb wildlife.

✿ Use the trail at your own risk.

✿ Leave only your thanks and footprints - take nothing but photographs.

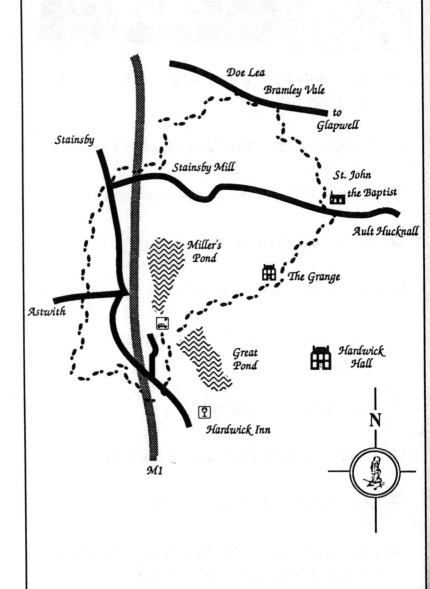

HARDWICK COUNTRY PARK
- 5 MILES
- allow 2 hours.

•• •• •• - *Hardwick Country Park Car Park - Astwith Lane - Stainsby Mill -Doe Lea - Bramley Vale - Hollingworth Wood - Hucknall Wood - Ault Hucknall Church - The Grange - Hardwick Country Park.*

- 1:25,000 Pathfinder Series Sheet No. SK 46/56 - Mansfield (North) and park of Sherwood Forest.

Hardwick Country Park. Grid Ref. SK453639.

None on the walk. Nearest 1/2 mile away at entrance to Hardwick Hall - Hardwick Inn.

ABOUT THE WALK - A beautiful walk taking you through Hardwick Country Park, past Stainsby Mill, through woodland and past the historic Ault Hucknall church. For more than half the walk the impressive Hardwick Hall and old hall dominate the landscape.

WALKING INSTRUCTIONS - From the car park turn left along the entrance road to the minor road and turn left to pass under the M1. 100 yards beyond the underpass is a footpath sign on your left. Turn left and ascend to the stile. Keep to the righthand side of the field to a stile at the top with woodland on your right. Continue ahead with the field boundary on your left for 100 yards towards a solitary tree. Turn right - almost back on yourself - and descend the field to a stile. Cross the next field aiming for the far lefthand corner with woodland on your left. Here is a stile and footpath sign. Cross Astwith Lane to another stile and footpath sign and walk along the righthand side of the fields all the way to the road near Stainsbybrook; reached via a stile. Turn left along the road and follow it round to your right and turn right; signed for Stainsby Mill. Walk under the M1 and continue along the road to Stainsby Mill and war memorial. Turn left up the no through road - Mill

Lane. You can cut this road walk out by turning left just after the underpass, at the footpath sign and walking around the field on the lefthand side to Mill Lane.

Near the end of the lane turn right, as footpath signed, and walk along the fenced path for 1/4 mile before turning right down a wide fenced track to a footbridge and ford. Cross the bridge and turn left along the tarmaced path towards Doe Lea. Ascends steps to the road and turn left towards the houses, turning right then left into East Street and reach Doe Lea Post Office. Turn right and gain the A617 road. Ascend it a few yards to the Bramley Vale sign and just after wards turn right onto the curving Bramley Road. Take the third road on your right, signed - Bramley Vale Primary School. Where it turns left keep straight on a footpath and follow it along the edge of Hollingworth Wood. In 1/4 mile follow the path round to your left and into Hucknall Wood. At the top of the wood coming out onto a track which you follow along the righthand side of the field to Hodmire Lane and Ault Hucknall church, dedicated to St. John the Baptist, on your left. The church is well worth visiting. Turn left then right along the bridlepath, a track, which in 1/2 mile reaches The Grange. Go through the bridlepath gate into Hardwick Country Park. The path is defined as you descend and swing to your right and cross a track to a gate. Continue descending and bear to your left to a gate and track. Turn right and soon reach the car park where you started.

HARDWICK HALL - One of the finest Elizabethan buildings in Britain and often referred to as "More glass than wall". The occupier and builder was the renowned Bess of Hardwick, the wife of George Talbot the sixth Earl of Shrewsbury. Work began in 1590 and seven years later she took up residence. The interior contains an extensive range of tapestries and is well known for its plasterwork in the Great Chamber and Long Gallery. The building is basically unaltered and each tower carries the bold initials ES - Elizabeth Shrewsbury. The building remained in the Cavendish family - the current Dukes of Devonshire - until 1959 when it was accepted in lieu of Death Duties and given to the National Trust.

AULT HUCKNALL CHURCH - dedicated to St. John the Baptist. In the outside walls can be seen carved stone from Norman and Saxon period. Inside is a monument to Anne Keighley, who died in 1627, the wife of the first Earl of Devonshire. Nearby is the monument to Thomas Hobbes, the philosopher who died in 1679 in Hardwick Hall. He was tutor to the Earls of Devonshire and to Charles 11.

Great Pond and Hardwick Hall - Old & New.

Ault Hucknall church & sculptures.

FIVE PITS TRAIL - 6 MILES

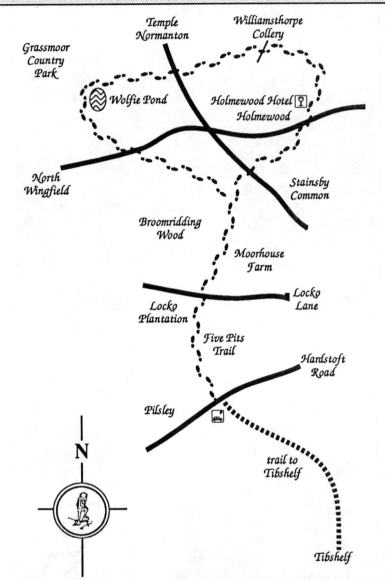

Temple
Normanton

Williamsthorpe
Colliery

Grassmoor
Country
Park

Wolfie Pond

Holmewood Hotel
Holmewood

North
Wingfield

Stainsby
Common

Broomridding
Wood

Moorhouse
Farm

Locko
Lane

Locko
Plantation

Five Pits
Trail

Hardstoft
Road

Pilsley

N

trail to
Tibshelf

Tibshelf

- *from opposite page* - left - signed Tibshelf. To the right the trail continue to Grassmoor and its Country Park. Follow the trail southwards and in 1/4 mile cross the road at Highfields. Just after the trail turns sharp left then right and in 1/4 mile regain the junction you reached in the early stages of the walk. Continue ahead and retrace your steps - about 1 1/2 miles - along the trail back to Hardstoft Road Picnic Site.

FIVE PITS TRAIL
- 6 MILES
- allow 2 or more hours.

•• •• •• *- Pilsley - Hardstoft Road Picnic Site - Five Pits Trail - Holmewood - Grassmoor - Hardstoft Road Picnic Site.*

 1:25,000 Pathfinder Series Sheet No. SK 46/56 - "Mansfield North and part of Sherwood Forest."

 - Hardstoft Road Picnic Site, Pilsley. Grid Ref. 429624.

 - Holmewood Hotel, Holmewood.

ABOUT THE WALK - This walk on the trail is a six mile circular one. The trail can be walked end to end - Tibshelf to Grassmoor - 6 miles or you could just do the circular walk from Grassmoor. There are many permutations. The trail was made between 1979 - 1989 by the Derbyshire County Council and basically joins together the collieries of Tibshelf, Pilsley, Williamthorpe, Holmewood and Grassmoor, together with three smaller ones - Alma, Pewit and Lings. The trail uses mineral lines in the north and sections of the "Great Central" line in the south. The walk is basically flat passing through surprisingly attractive countryside, past farms, fields with crops and sheep; the views west to the Peakland hills is extensive.

WALKING INSTRUCTIONS - Starting from the Hardstoft Road Picnic Site on the eastern side of Pilsley, cross the road and start walking along the Five Pits Trail. In 1/2 mile pass Locko Plantation and descend to Locko Lane. Cross over and continue along the trail and in a further 1/2 mile pass Broomridding Wood and reach Timber Lane. Bear right to continue along the trail with Timber Lane Picnic site on your left. Continue on the trail for just over 1/4 mile to a fork in the trail. The one on your left to Grassmoor, is your return route. Keep to the right one, to Holmewood. This soon crosses a road and continue on to the main road in Holmewood. Cross over and walk along the road past the rows of houses and Holmewood Hotel to a path sign and descend to a road, with a major distribution centre on your left. Ascend the other side and turn left, continuing on the trail again. In 1/2 mile descend a "steep slope" and follow the trail round to your left and in 1/4 mile pass the winding gear of Williamthorpe Colliery. Just afterwards is a side trail to Temple Normanton. Continue and walk under a road and and follow the trail to Wolfie Pond; a popular fishing place. Here turn

ASHOVER & KELSTEDGE
- 8 MILES

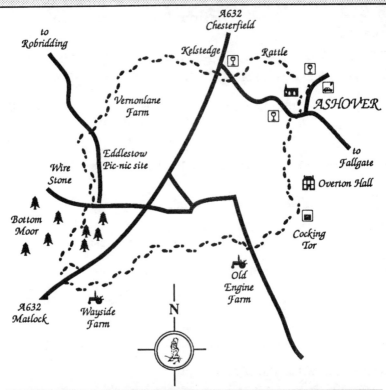

Crispin Inn, Ashover.

ASHOVER
&
KELSTEDGE
- 8 MILES

- allow 3 hours.

- Ashover - Overton - Cocking Tor - Old Engine Farm - Wayside Farm - Bottom Moor Forest - Eddlestow Picnic site - Vernon Lane - Kelstedge - Marsh Green - Rattle - Ashover.

 - 1:25,000 Pathfinder Series Sheet No. 778 (SK 26/36) - Bakewell & Matlock.

- Ashover by Parish Hall. Eddlestow Picnic site, Grid Ref. SK324634.

- Black Swan, Crispin Inn, Red Lion Inn, Ashover. Kelstedge Inn, Kelstedge.

ABOUT THE WALK - Ashover is a particularly interesting village with an impressive church and historical inn. The walk takes you first to Overton and its impressive hall before ascending again, steeply, to the wooded edge of Cocking Tor. From here you cross fields to Wayside Farm and forest of Bottom Moor. After walking through the pine plantation you begin descending to Kelstedge. From here you return to Ashover via Marsh Green and Rattle. One of the longest walks in this book but a firm favourite of mine and one that I never tire of walking, whatever the season.

WALKING INSTRUCTIONS - From the car park turn left along the main road past the Black Swan Inn, Crispin Inn and church to the road junction infront of the Red Lion at the bottom. Turn left then right down the track by the inn. At the bottom cross the bridge over the River Amber and start ascending. Where it turns right use the stile on your left and continue ascending along a stone flagged path to a stile and track. Continue ahead on the track - now level - to a junction with Overton Hall to your left. Cross over to a path and follow this round and above Overton Cottages. Continue through woodland gently ascending to an old mining area. Here turn right and ascend more steeply keeping the edge of the woodland on your right to the top of the edge - Cocking Tor. Keep straight ahead with the wall on your immediate left to reach a stile. Cross the field beyond aiming for the immediate lefthand side of a circular walled plantation. Continue to the far righthand corner of the field to a stile, footpath sign, and road.

Turn right for a few yards, passing Old Engine Farm on your left, to a stile and footpath sign on your left. Turn left and descend the field to a stile and on past a small lake and ruined wind pump, to a stile. Keep the wall on your right to another stile then cross a field to another and continue descending to a further stile. Here continue ahead with the field boundary on your left to a stile with a thin plantation on your left. Continue beside the wall to a minor road. Cross over and continue on the well stiled path across three fields to an arm of Lantlodge Wood. Go straight through to a stile and onto another with buildings on your left. A few yards further turn right across the field aiming for the righthand side of Wayside Farm (caravan site). Walk through the farm to the A632 road, with footpath sign - "Ashover".

Turn left then right onto a track, footpath signed - "Rushley & Robridding". A few yards along here turn right again at the stile and path sign - "Robridding". The path keeps close to a wall on your right with forest on your left. After a short distance the path bears left and for little over the next 1/2 mile you walk through the forest keeping straight ahead at all forest breaks, to reach a stile and road junction at Eddlestow Lot, near the Wire Stone. Go straight across and descend the road passing Eddlestow Picnic site and car park on your right. 1/4 mile later the road turns sharp left; here turn right onto a track and descend Vernon Lane. At the entrance gates to Vernonlane Farm bear left on the path and follow it down into woodland and cross Hodgelane Brook via a stone slab bridge. Continue onto another over Smalley Brook. The path soon becomes a lane as you enter Kelstedge. Cross the A632 road and walk up the road past Kelstedge Inn on your left. At the Ashover road turn right for a few yards to a track on your left; footpath signed. Turn left along this crossing Marsh Brook and onto the houses of Marsh Green. Bear right, now on a tarmaced surface to the road in Rattle. Turn right along it back to Ashover and the Black Swan Inn. Turn left back to the car park.

OVERTON HALL - former home of Sir Joseph Banks, the naturalist who went with Captain Cook in the Endeavour.

ASHOVER - Once an important lead mining area. Gregory Mine averaged 511 tons of ore a year between 1728-1806. The church, dedicated to All Saints, has many interesting tombs and brasses. The 15th century tower and spire were built by the Babington family, who lived at Dethick south-east of Matlock. The lead font is a rare feature and is one of about thirty to be seen in Britain. It was made from local lead in about 1150 and illustrates twenty men standing under arches and holding books. The chancel has several monuments - to Philip Eyre; James Rolleston and Thomas Babington who died in 1518.

Ashover.

Cheese press, Kelstedge.

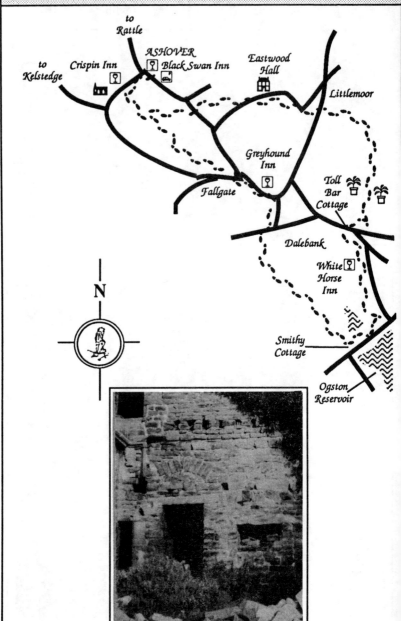

to
Rattle

to
Kelstedge

Crispin Inn

ASHOVER
Black Swan Inn

Eastwood
Hall

Littlemoor

Greyhound
Inn

Toll
Bar
Cottage

Fallgate

Dalebank

White
Horse
Inn

N

Smithy
Cottage

Ogston
Reservoir

Ruins of Eastwood Hall.

ASHOVER AND OGSTON RESERVOIR - 6 MILES

- allow 2 1/4 hours.

- Ashover - Hockley Quarry - Fall Hill - Fallgate - *Smithy Cottage - Ogston Reservoir - Woolley Moor - Woodhead Farm - Littlemoor - Eastwood Hall - Ashover.*

 1:25,000 Pathfinder Series Sheet No.761 (SK 36/37) - Chesterfield.

 - Ashover by Parish Hall.

Black Swan, Crispin Inn, Ashover; Greyhound Inn, Fallgate; White Horse Inn, Woolley Moor.

ABOUT THE WALK - A beautiful walk across fields and woodland, past historical inns to Ogston Reservoir. You return to Ashover through Woolley Moor and past an old Toll Bar Cottage and impressive chrysanthium garden centre, to cross fields to Woodhead Farm. Here following a little used right of way you gain Littlemoor and descend to the ruins of Eastwood Hall before regaining your starting out path from Ashover.

WALKING INSTRUCTIONS - From the car park in Ashover turn left down the main street past the Swan Inn to opposite the Crispin Inn. Here turn left along a walled path on the right of an impressive mullioned building. The path is well defined and stiled and after 1/4 mile becomes just a path with a wall on your right, then left. Further left you can see the ruins of Eastwood Hall and that is your return route to this path. Continue on the path and follow it round to your right to woodland and a quarry on your left. Continue through the woodland and bear right and descend with the quarry on your right and descend steps to the minor road - B6036. Turn left through Fallgate to the 17th century Greyhound Inn. Here turn right onto the single lane road and follow it to a road junction. Here go straight across onto a tarmaced walled path and descend to a footbridge. Continue up the otherside to another minor road. Here turn left and follow it for 1/4 mile to another road junction. Again go straight across and walk along a track which soon becomes a well stiled path. In a 1/3 mile walk through a small wood and continue to the B6014 road beside Smithy Cottage on your left. As you walked you will have seen Woolley Moor on your left which you will be walking through soon. Infront of you is Ogston Reservoir and turn left.

Cross the arm of the reservoir to the first road on your left - White Horse Lane. Turn left and ascend the road past the White Horse Inn and bear left along Badger Lane in Woolley Moor to the road junction - B6036 - with the Toll Bar Cottage on your right and Rileys Chrysanthiums beyond. Turn right and after a few yards close to the righthand corner of the gardens is a stone stile on your left. Go through this and keep to the edge of the field and soon bear right to a stile. Cross over a small ditch and turn left keeping the field boundary on your left with the chrysanthiums beyond. The path is defined and stiled. Once past the perimeter of the gardens aim for the bottom righthand corner of the field where there is a stile. Walk around the next field, keeping the field boundary on your right to a stile and track to Woodhead Farm. Follow the track to the outskirts of the farm to a small pond. Turn left through a stile near the gate and descend the field to the far righthand corner to a stile. Cross the next field towards its middle to a wooden stile and woodland. Walk through and continue straight ahead ascending the field to a stile and Ashover Road on the left of Littlemoor. Go straight across to a stile and follow the path beside the wall with a house on your right to a stile. Continue in woodland curving to your right to another stile and lane. Turn left and descend the lane to the ruins of Eastwood Hall. Turn right along the track on the left of the house and ruins to a gate and stile. Turn left and walk along the field edge to stiles and minor road from Ashover. Turn right and towards the end of the second field on your left, turn left through a stile and cross the field to another. At the end of the next field regain your starting out path and turn right and retrace your steps back to the Crispin Inn and turn right along the road back to the car park.

OGSTON RESERVOIR - Made in 1958 and covering 206 acres. The most popular bird spotting place in Derbyshire with more than 200 species sighted.

EASTWOOD HALL - Shorty before the Civil War, the hall was purchased by the Rev. Immanuel Bourne, who became the vicar. With the outbreak of the war he remained neutral, which pleased neither side. Eventually he sided with the Parliamentarians but they did not trust him and as a result destroyed his home. So hard was it to demolish that they eventually had to use gunpowder.

Toll bar Cottage, Woolley Moor.

Ogston Reservoir.

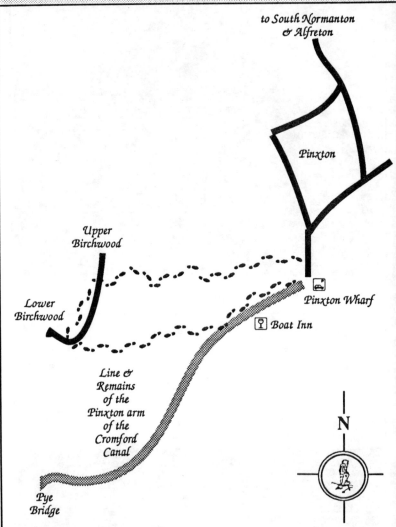

to South Normanton
& Alfreton

Pinxton

Upper
Birchwood

Lower
Birchwood

Pinxton Wharf

Boat Inn

Line &
Remains
of the
Pinxton arm
of the
Cromford
Canal

Pye
Bridge

N

PINXTON CANAL - The Pinxton Arm of the Cromford Canal was surveyed and designed by William Jessop in the 1790's. Originally it was planned to continue the canal towards Mansfield and its collieries but it would have required a huge flight of locks to Kirby summit. Instead a tramway was built in 1819 to carry the coal to Pinxton Wharf. From the Boat Inn, here, in 1830 a tram left every Thursday for Mansfield Market. The tram was known as "Eppersons' Coach", after the landlord of the inn. As a result the Boat Inn can claim to be the first passenger railway station in Derbyshire!

PINXTON
- 3 MILES
- allow 1 hour.

- Pinxton - Pinxton Canal - Lower Birchwood - Upper Birchwood - Pinxton.

1:25,000 Pathfinder Series Sheet No. 795 (SK 45/55) - Sutton in Ashfield.

- Pinxton Wharf (roadside parking only) at Grid Ref. SK 454544. Reached via Wharf Road and Alexander Terrace.

- Boat Inn, Pinxton Canal.

ABOUT THE WALK - A short one basically to visit and see Pinxton Wharf, the terminus of the now abandoned Pinxton Canal, an arm of the Cromford Canal, which it leaves at Ironville. Here right on the Derbyshire/Nottinghamshire boundary is a little haven. The walk takes along the canal before following a track to Lower Birchwood. Here a short road walk brings you to the path back to Pinxton and its canal.

WALKING INSTRUCTIONS - Walk either on the righthand side or left of the canal - both join near the Boat Inn. Continue on the lefthand side of the canal and pass the Boat Inn. Upto now the canal has been waterfilled and well defined but just ahead it became reed filled and then lost. Continue you to a track and follow this close to the line of the canal. Pass a scrap yard on your right and continue on the track which soon bears right and passes under a railway. Continue on the track and pass under another railway line before gaining the road and houses at Lower Birchwood. Turn right along the minor road and cross a railway line. 200 yards later the road turns left and on the bend is the stile and footpath sign - Pinxton 1 1/4 miles. Turn right over the stile and through woodland to another stile on your left. Keep the field boundary on your right and reach another stile and a road. Cross over to a stile and turn right along a fenced path. After a short distance turn left and follow a well defined hedged path. This brings into a field where keep ahead on the righthand side of the field to reach a track. Turn left along it to reach Pinxton where turn right to regain Pinxton Wharf.

WALK RECORD CHART

date walked

THE MOSS VALLEY & ECKINGTON - 5 MILES ....

HOLMESFIELD & CORDWELL - 6 MILES ....

OLD WHITTINGTON & UNSTONE - 6 MILES ....

CRESWELL CRAGS - 3 MILES ....

THE CRESWELL ARCHAEOLOGICAL WAY - 13 MILES ....

LINACRE RESERVOIRS & OLD BRAMPTON - 4 MILES ....

CHESTERFIELD & THE CHESTERFIELD CANAL - 4 1/2 MILES .....

HOLYMOORSIDE & STANDEDGE - 4 MILES ....

BOLSOVER & SCARCLIFFE - 4 1/2 MILES ....

HARDWICK COUNTRY PARK - 5 MILES ....

FIVE PITS TRAIL - 6 MILES ....

ASHOVER & KELSTEDGE - 8 MILES ....

ASHOVER & OGSTON RESERVOIR - 6 MILES ....

PINXTON - 3 MILES ....

THE JOHN MERRILL WALK BADGE - complete six of these walks and send details together with £2.75 for a special circular embroidered badge and signed certificate - to Trail Crest Publications .
"I'VE DONE A JOHN MERRTILL WALK" T SHIRT - green with white lettering and logo. £7.50 from Trail Crest Publications Ltd.

"from footprint to finished book"

OTHER BOOKS by John N. Merrill Published by TRAIL CREST PUBLICATIONS Ltd.

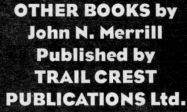

CIRCULAR WALK GUIDES -

SHORT CIRCULAR WALKS IN THE PEAK DISTRICT - Vol. 1 and 2
CIRCULAR WALKS IN WESTERN PEAKLAND
SHORT CIRCULAR WALKS IN THE STAFFORDSHIRE MOORLANDS
SHORT CIRCULAR WALKS - TOWNS & VILLAGES OF THE PEAK DISTRICT
SHORT CIRCULAR WALKS AROUND MATLOCK
SHORT CIRCULAR WALKS IN THE DUKERIES
SHORT CIRCULAR WALKS IN SOUTH YORKSHIRE
SHORT CIRCULAR WALKS IN SOUTH DERBYSHIRE
SHORT CIRCULAR WALKS AROUND BUXTON
SHORT CIRCULAR WALKS AROUND WIRKSWORTH
SHORT CIRCULAR WALKS IN THE HOPE VALLEY
10 SHORT CIRCULAR WALKS IN THE PEAK DISTRICT
CIRCULAR WALKS ON KINDER & BLEAKLOW
SHORT CIRCULAR WALKS IN SOUTH NOTTINGHAMSHIRE
SHIRT CIRCULAR WALKS IN CHESHIRE
SHORT CIRCULAR WALKS IN WEST YORKSHIRE
CIRCULAR WALKS TO PEAK DISTRICT AIRCRAFT WRECKS by John Mason
CIRCULAR WALKS IN THE DERBYSHIRE DALES
SHORT CIRCULAR WALKS IN EAST DEVON
SHORT CIRCULAR WALKS AROUND HARROGATE
SHORT CIRCULAR WALKS IN CHARNWOOD FOREST
SHORT CIRCULAR WALKS AROUND CHESTERFIELD
SHORT CIRCULAR WALKS IN THE YORKS DALES - Vol 1 - Southern area.
SHORT CIRCULAR WALKS IN THE AMBER VALLEY (Derbyshire)
SHORT CIRCULAR WALKS IN THE LAKE DISTRICT
SHORT CIRCULAR WALKS IN EAST STAFFORDSHIRE
LONG CIRCULAR WALKS IN THE PEAK DISTRICT - Vol.1 and 2.
LONG CIRCULAR WALKS IN THE STAFFORDSHIRE MOORLANDS
LONG CIRCULAR WALKS IN CHESHIRE
WALKING THE TISSINGTON TRAIL
WALKING THE HIGH PEAK TRAIL

CANAL WALKS -

VOL 1 - DERBYSHIRE & NOTTINGHAMSHIRE
VOL 2 - CHESHIRE & STAFFORDSHIRE
VOL 3 - STAFFORDSHIRE
VOL 4 - THE CHESHIRE RING
VOL 5 - LINCOLNSHIRE & NOTTINGHAMSHIRE
VOL 6 - SOUTH YORKSHIRE
VOL 7 - THE TRENT & MERSEY CANAL

JOHN MERRILL DAY CHALLENGE WALKS -

WHITE PEAK CHALLENGE WALK
DARK PEAK CHALLENGE WALK
PEAK DISTRICT END TO END WALKS
STAFFORDSHIRE MOORLANDS CHALLENGE WALK
THE LITTLE JOHN CHALLENGE WALK

YORKSHIRE DALES CHALLENGE WALK
NORTH YORKSHIRE MOORS CHALLENGE WALK
LAKELAND CHALLENGE WALK
THE RUTLAND WATER CHALLENGE WALK
MALVERN HILLS CHALLENGE WALK
THE SALTER'S WAY
THE SNOWDON CHALLENGE
CHARNWOOD FOREST CHALLENGE WALK
THREE COUNTIES CHALLENGE WALK (Peak District).

INSTRUCTION & RECORD -
HIKE TO BE FIT.....STROLLING WITH JOHN
THE JOHN MERRILL WALK RECORD BOOK

MULTIPLE DAY WALKS -
THE RIVERS'S WAY
PEAK DISTRICT: HIGH LEVEL ROUTE
PEAK DISTRICT MARATHONS
THE LIMEY WAY
THE PEAKLAND WAY

COAST WALKS & NATIONAL TRAILS -
ISLE OF WIGHT COAST PATH
PEMBROKESHIRE COAST PATH
THE CLEVELAND WAY
WALKING ANGELSEY'S COASTLINE.

PEAK DISTRICT HISTORICAL GUIDES -
A to Z GUIDE OF THE PEAK DISTRICT
DERBYSHIRE INNS - an A to Z guide
HALLS AND CASTLES OF THE PEAK DISTRICT & DERBYSHIRE
TOURING THE PEAK DISTRICT & DERBYSHIRE BY CAR
DERBYSHIRE FOLKLORE
PUNISHMENT IN DERBYSHIRE
CUSTOMS OF THE PEAK DISTRICT & DERBYSHIRE
WINSTER - a souvenir guide
ARKWRIGHT OF CROMFORD
LEGENDS OF DERBYSHIRE
DERBYSHIRE FACTS & RECORDS
TALES FROM THE MINES by Geoffrey Carr
PEAK DISTRICT PLACE NAMES by Martin Spray

> for a free copy
> of the
> **John Merrill**
> **Walk Guide**
> Catalogue
> write to -
> Trail Crest Publications Ltd.

JOHN MERRILL'S MAJOR WALKS -
TURN RIGHT AT LAND'S END
WITH MUSTARD ON MY BACK
TURN RIGHT AT DEATH VALLEY
EMERALD COAST WALK

SKETCH BOOKS -
SKETCHES OF THE PEAK DISTRICT

COLOUR BOOK:-
THE PEAK DISTRICT......something to remember her by.

OVERSEAS GUIDES -
HIKING IN NEW MEXICO - Vol I - The Sandia and Manzano Mountains.
Vol 2 - Hiking "Billy the Kid" Country. Vol 4 - N.W. area - " Hiking Indian Country."
"WALKING IN DRACULA COUNTRY" - Romania.